enjoy camping

written & illustrated by

doug mountford

The Scout Association
Baden-Powell House,
Queen's Gate,
London SW7 5JS

Copyright © 1973
Doug Mountford

SBN 85165 087 2

First Edition **July 1973**

Sixth Printing **July 1977**

Printed in England by
Kent Paper Company Ltd, London and Ashford, Kent.

Contents

Foreword

Camping is a basic Scouting activity. One of the first things you will learn, as a Scout, is to look after yourself in the open.

If, later on, you decide to do a long-distance hike, sleeping each night at a different place, you should be able to pitch camp without delay or difficulty, no matter what the weather. You should learn how best to pack your gear, light a fire, cook, keep warm and dry, and how to survive, if necessary, on a minimum of supplies and equipment.

You will have these skills explained to you at Troop and Patrol Meetings in the winter so that you are ready to practise them at camps throughout the rest of the year.

You can use camp as a base for other activities such as climbing, gliding or sailing—and the more you learn about camping the more you will enjoy it. The purpose of this book is to show through the illustrations some of the enjoyment of camping; to suggest to Patrol Leaders ideas they may like to adopt for their own Patrols and to provide beginners with an idea of how a Scout camp operates. However, you won't learn everything about camp from these pages. First Aid, catering, cooking, the Country Code and religious observance are all dealt with at length in other publications, and would more than double the cost of a book which is intended to supplement the Patrol Leader's instruction rather than supplant it. It should be used in conjunction with other material, such as SCOUTING magazine wall charts and *Scout Camping* by Tony Kemp and Jeremy Sutton-Pratt.

Before going to camp you must carefully plan your programme, otherwise you may start a project at camp, only to find that you haven't brought all the necessary equipment to complete it. Long before camp you will be dreaming about the adventures you will have at camp, so turn the dreams to good account by writing a list of the things you want to do, and making drawings or models. Get the rest of your Patrol to do the same, so that when the Patrol Leader calls a council to work out the programme for camp there will be plenty of good ideas to discuss—instead of a deafening silence. The Patrol Leader will then start looking for a suitable camp site, and preparing for the activities you have decided to attempt. But don't expect him to do it all himself. He will get all his Patrol to assist in the preparations, perhaps by writing a letter or two to Camp Wardens or landowners; by overhauling equipment; by shopping for supplies. While helping with these preparations you will learn how a camp is run. So that when you go off camping with a friend, you will have confidence in your own ability to manage as a completely independent unit.

A Note to Patrol Leaders

This book is designed to help you run camps with your Patrol, by giving the Scouts an idea of the possibilities and problems they may encounter under canvas.

Discuss with them what they want to do at camp, and talk about the charts in this book. In this way it should be possible to foresee any difficulties that might arise, and plan to avoid them.

The more the Scouts know about camp life, the more they will feel at home when they actually get there. The story of the Scout who complained that there was nowhere to sleep as the tent had no 'upstairs', is nearer to reality than some of us would care to believe. The prospect of using an earth latrine can be quite a shock to a boy who vaguely assumed that there would be flush toilets. Of course, you will have explained all these things at a Patrol Meeting and the Scout Leader will also have mentioned them. But if the Scout in question happened to be away or out of the room at the time a glance through this book may help to fill some of the gaps in his knowledge.

Involve all the members of your Patrol in planning the camp from the beginning. Talk about the personal gear the Scouts hope to bring, so that you don't turn up for your lightweight hike-camp to find that someone has decided to bring their double bass along with them!

If you are not already in the habit of running regular Patrol Camps, get the Scout Leader to go with you when you visit the parents of your Scouts—to introduce you and set their minds at rest about their son's safety while in your charge. It is also a good idea to involve your Leader in preparing forms for the parents to sign, giving permission for their sons to attend camp. You are much less likely to be let down by a new Scout if the parents have been kept fully informed, and if documents reach them on properly headed Group paper.

On page 32 you will see an illustration of the Patrol Camping Award. To gain the Award, you must have camped, as a Patrol, for a minimum of nine nights within a period of a year on at least three separate occasions. Obtain details from your local Scout Shop.

Don't imagine that because you see something in a book it must be right, or that printed instructions should ever be followed blindly. If you see a camp site layout arranged in a certain way try to understand why this has been done and adapt it to your particular circumstances. The central wash place and wet pit shown on the centre pages is hygienically sound only on soil which drains easily and in reasonably fair weather. On a clay soil it could well become a pleasant wallowing-hole for your pet hippo!

Troop camp should not become an open-air prison, but a centre for exploring the country around you, and attempting all the activities that can't be done at home. Practise hike-camping and canoeing and use any facilities for other activities such as gliding or climbing, which may be available in the area. Another year you may decide to run a camp that is continually on the move—there are some suggestions for more adventurous forms of camping at the back of the book.

Now it only remains for me to wish you—GOOD CAMPING!

Patrol Camp Gear

WHAT YOUR PATROL TAKES TO CAMP WILL DEPEND ON THE KIND OF PROGRAMME YOU HOPE TO TAKE PART IN. THE FOLLOWING LIST COVERS MOST OF THE THINGS LIKELY TO BE WANTED FOR GENERAL USE BY THE PATROL

Main Site Equipment
Patrol Tent, groundsheet, poles, guys, pegs;
Cooking and dining shelters, poles, guys, pegs;
Sisal and rope for gadgets (See page 18);
Patrol Box converting to table;
Handaxe or Bushsaw;
Flags, halliards, flag pole.

Equipment for latrines
Lat. screens, poles, guys, pegs;
Toilet paper in waterproof container, trowel;
Washbowl, soap, towel;
Pick-axe, shovel.

Cooking Equipment
Large dixie, teapot,
Nest of billies,
Frying pan,
Water carriers,
Baking and serving dish,
Wooden spoon, soup ladle,
Kitchen knife, fork, fish slice,
Tin opener, bottle opener,
Plastic bags, aluminium foil,
Pudding cloth, butter muslin,
Paraffin stove or gas stove,
Paraffin and meths, or spare gas cylinders,
Matches in waterproof container,
Axe and pruning saw for firewood,
Food as required by agreed menu.

Washing and Washing-up Equipment
Washbowls, bucket,
Washing-up liquid or powder,
Dish cloth, tea towel,
Mop and scrubbing brush,
Plastic plate rack.

Emergency Equipment
First Aid box, properly stocked.
Spare airbed, blankets,
Lamp and torch.

Special Activity and Games Equipment
Take whatever your programme requires.
Don't forget emergency rations and life-saving equipment.

General Neatness
Handbrush and pan, sponge,
Boot brush and polish,
Mirror, clothes brush,
Suitcase for storing uniforms.

Personal Camp Gear

IT IS NICE TO LOOK FORWARD TO THE ADVENTURES YOU ARE GOING TO HAVE AT CAMP. A DAY OR TWO BEFORE YOU SET OUT PUT THIS DAYDREAMING TO PRACTICAL USE BY DRESSING UP FOR EACH ACTIVITY IN TURN AND MAKING SURE YOU HAVE ALL YOU NEED. AS YOU TAKE OFF EACH SET OF GEAR, PACK IT IN YOUR RUCSAC READY FOR CAMP.

Uniform (to be worn)
Beret, scarf, trousers, Scout belt, Scout shirt and/or jersey, socks, shoes, outer garment. Passport if you are going abroad.

In-Camp Wear
Heavy jeans for rough wear, old shirt, warm sweater, waterproof coat, camp shoes, strong boots or shoes.

Change of clothes
Spare socks, shirt, trousers, underclothes, handkerchiefs.

Activity Wear
Complete set of kit appropriate to activity to be undertaken.

Night time
Groundsheet, sleeping bag, pyjamas, polythene bags for keeping gear dry. Lilo or camp bed only if Patrol all agree there is room, torch.

Morning
Soap, flannel, comb, toothbrush, toothpaste in waterproof bag. Swimming trunks and towel for your morning dip.

Meal times
Mug, two unbreakable dishes, knife, fork, spoon, teaspoon in bag, tea towel.

Spare time
Progress book, notebook, biro, pencil, mending materials.

Off colour
Personal First Aid kit to fit pocket.

MARK EVERYTHING WITH YOUR NAME AND PACK IN RUCSAC MARKED WITH YOUR NAME. TAKE NO MORE THAN YOU NEED — YOU WILL HAVE TO CARRY IT ALL YOURSELF !

6

Pitching a Ridge Tent

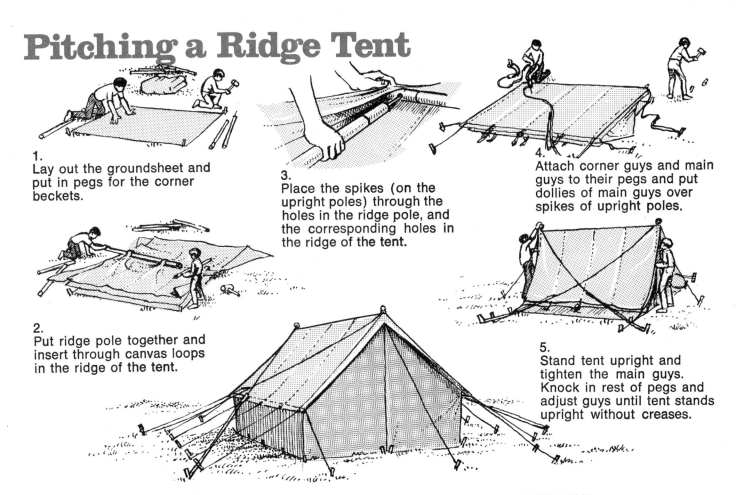

1.
Lay out the groundsheet and put in pegs for the corner beckets.

2.
Put ridge pole together and insert through canvas loops in the ridge of the tent.

3.
Place the spikes (on the upright poles) through the holes in the ridge pole, and the corresponding holes in the ridge of the tent.

4.
Attach corner guys and main guys to their pegs and put dollies of main guys over spikes of upright poles.

5.
Stand tent upright and tighten the main guys. Knock in rest of pegs and adjust guys until tent stands upright without creases.

PRACTISE ERECTING YOUR TENT WELL BEFORE YOU GO TO CAMP.

Pitching a Hike Tent

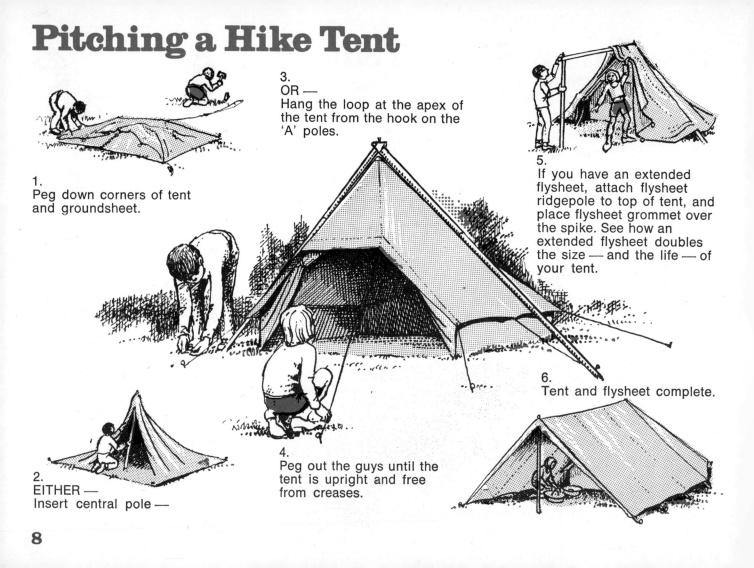

1.
Peg down corners of tent and groundsheet.

2.
EITHER —
Insert central pole —

3.
OR —
Hang the loop at the apex of the tent from the hook on the 'A' poles.

4.
Peg out the guys until the tent is upright and free from creases.

5.
If you have an extended flysheet, attach flysheet ridgepole to top of tent, and place flysheet grommet over the spike. See how an extended flysheet doubles the size — and the life — of your tent.

6.
Tent and flysheet complete.

Pitching a Frame Tent

A. EXTERNAL FRAME

1.
Lay out the tent and put together the upper section of the frame on top of it. Insert all the brailing pegs.

2.
Attach loops on tent to hooks on top of frame. The flysheet, if any, may be laid over the frame at this stage.

3.
Straighten the legs of the frame so that the centre of the tent is upright. Assemble and attach the supports for the tent ends.

4.
Lift outwards the base of the tent-end supports until the whole tent is erect. Then open up the flysheet.

5.
Attach the flysheet poles and guys.

B. INTERNAL FRAME

Internal frames also should be half erected when the canvas is put on, but any inner tents are hung inside later.

ON THESE THREE PAGES WE HAVE SHOWN WAYS OF PITCHING THREE COMMON TYPES OF TENT.

THERE ARE MANY VARIATIONS IN DESIGN, HOWEVER, SO ALWAYS READ THE INSTRUCTIONS ISSUED BY THE TENT MAKERS.

Preparing Firewood

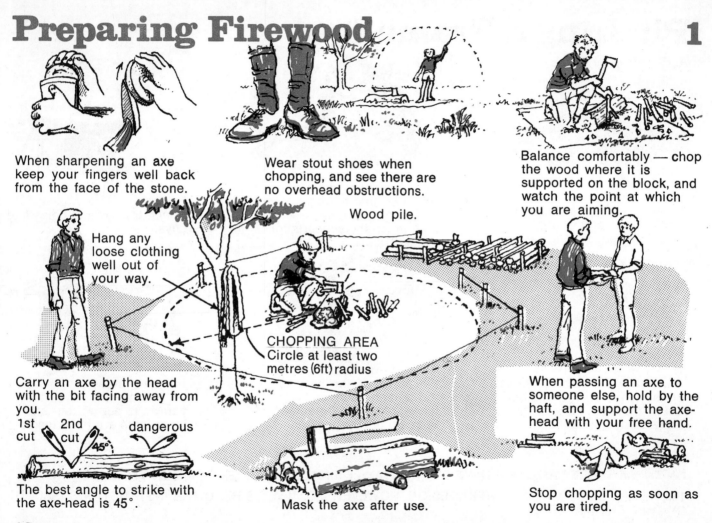

When sharpening an **axe** keep your fingers well back from the face of the stone.

Wear stout shoes when chopping, and see there are no overhead obstructions.

Balance comfortably — chop the wood where it is supported on the block, and watch the point at which you are aiming.

Wood pile.

Hang any loose clothing well out of your way.

CHOPPING AREA
Circle at least two metres (6ft) radius

Carry an axe by the head with the bit facing away from you.

1st cut   2nd cut   dangerous
45°

The best angle to strike with the axe-head is 45°.

Mask the axe after use.

When passing an axe to someone else, hold by the haft, and support the axe-head with your free hand.

Stop chopping as soon as you are tired.

Preparing Firewood

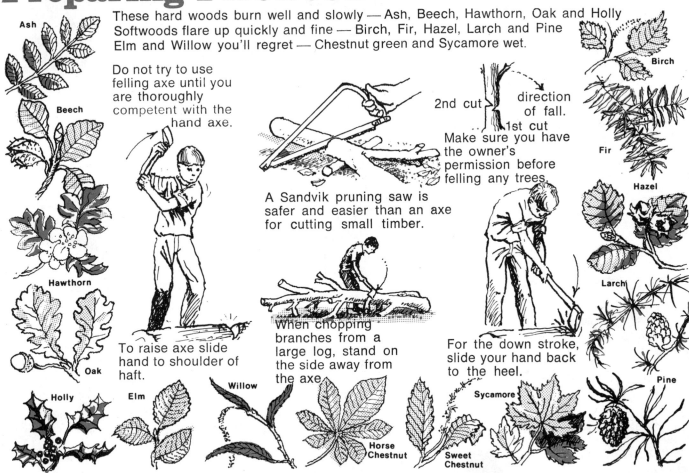

These hard woods burn well and slowly — Ash, Beech, Hawthorn, Oak and Holly
Softwoods flare up quickly and fine — Birch, Fir, Hazel, Larch and Pine
Elm and Willow you'll regret — Chestnut green and Sycamore wet.

Ash

Beech

Hawthorn

Oak

Holly

Elm

Willow

Birch

Fir

Hazel

Larch

Pine

Horse Chestnut

Sweet Chestnut

Sycamore

Do not try to use felling axe until you are thoroughly competent with the hand axe.

A Sandvik pruning saw is safer and easier than an axe for cutting small timber.

2nd cut   direction of fall.
1st cut
Make sure you have the owner's permission before felling any trees.

To raise axe slide hand to shoulder of haft.

When chopping branches from a large log, stand on the side away from the axe.

For the down stroke, slide your hand back to the heel.

Fire Lighting

1.
Pick kindling wood from near the base of dry hawthorn, birch or fir trees. Clear the turf from an area a metre square, and store turves in a damp place.

2.
Stand first twig upright in ground. If earth is damp first lay down a sheet of metal foil.

3.
Stand finest kindling thickly around upright.

4.
Stand very thin twigs thickly around the kindling, leaving a gap for the match on the windward side.

5.
Light your match, shielding the flame in your hand.

6.
Light the kindling. Add more tiny twigs, as necessary to each flame until it spreads to the thicker wood.
If you need to blow the fire, get in close.

7.
Place logs either side of fire to channel draught and to support grids, dixies etc. Cook on hot embers, NOT over the yellow flame.

Types of Cooking Fire

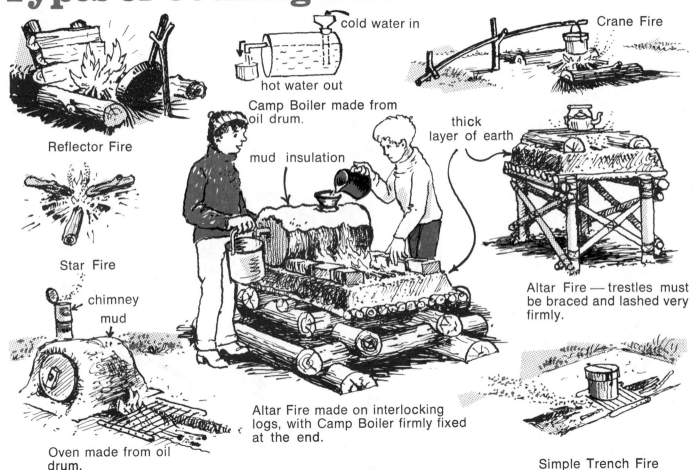

Reflector Fire

Star Fire

chimney

mud

Oven made from oil drum.

cold water in

hot water out

Camp Boiler made from oil drum.

mud insulation

Altar Fire made on interlocking logs, with Camp Boiler firmly fixed at the end.

Crane Fire

thick layer of earth

Altar Fire — trestles must be braced and lashed very firmly.

Simple Trench Fire

13

Pressure Stoves

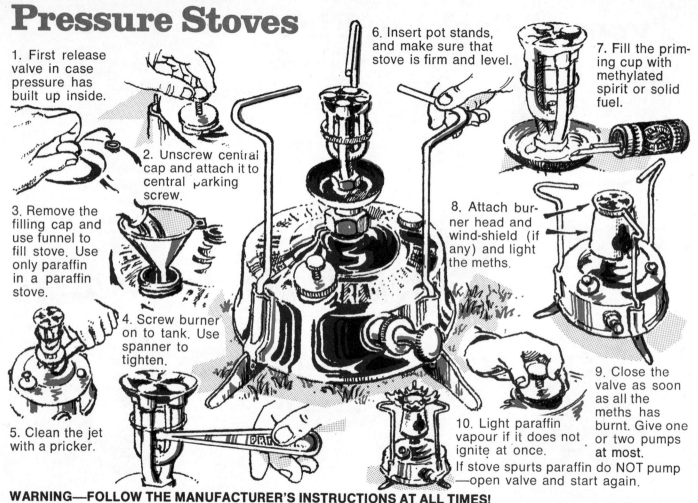

1. First release valve in case pressure has built up inside.

2. Unscrew central cap and attach it to central parking screw.

3. Remove the filling cap and use funnel to fill stove. Use only paraffin in a paraffin stove.

4. Screw burner on to tank. Use spanner to tighten.

5. Clean the jet with a pricker.

6. Insert pot stands, and make sure that stove is firm and level.

7. Fill the priming cup with methylated spirit or solid fuel.

8. Attach burner head and wind-shield (if any) and light the meths.

9. Close the valve as soon as all the meths has burnt. Give one or two pumps at most.

10. Light paraffin vapour if it does not ignite at once. If stove spurts paraffin do NOT pump—open valve and start again.

WARNING—FOLLOW THE MANUFACTURER'S INSTRUCTIONS AT ALL TIMES!

Gas Stoves

1. Disposable gas containers should be changed outside the tent, away from naked lights. Shake first to make sure they are empty and turn tap hard off.

2. Unscrew the burner completely before removing the cartridge.

3. Unscrew the base or other retaining device.

4. Place empty containers in a sack, well away from the tent.

5. Insert new cartridge and close the base firmly before screwing back burner.

6. Make sure that the stove is firm and level. Hold lighted match to burner while you turn on the gas.

7. If you must cook in tent:—keep door open; stand stove on flat stone by door; boil rather than fry food; anyone else in tent must keep still.

WARNING—FOLLOW THE MANUFACTURER'S INSTRUCTIONS AT ALL TIMES!

Next Patrol—out of sight and earshot

Mug rack

Dining area

Woodpile

Water

Cooking area

Chopping area

Gas outside

food cov

Soap

Trench fire

Oven

PREVAILING WIND

THIS WAY TO LATRINES

Patro
in A

16

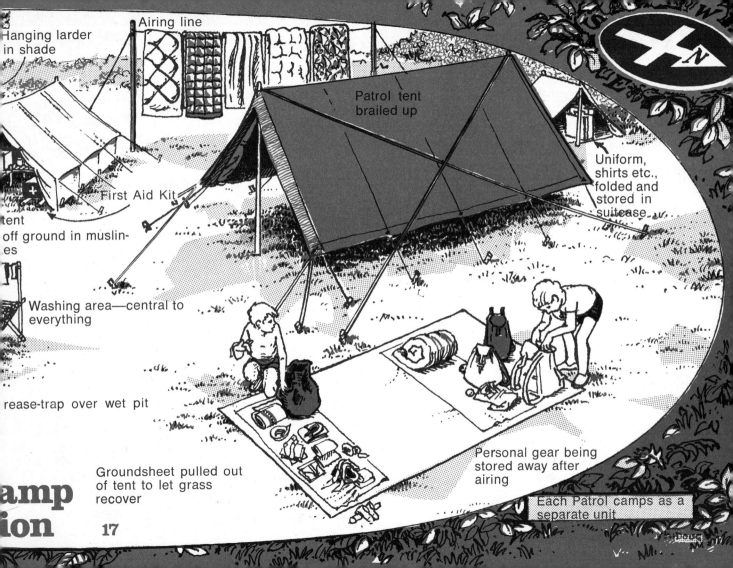

Hanging larder in shade

Airing line

Patrol tent brailed up

First Aid Kit

tent off ground in muslines

Uniform, shirts etc., folded and stored in suitcase

Washing area—central to everything

rease-trap over wet pit

Groundsheet pulled out of tent to let grass recover

Personal gear being stored away after airing

amp
ion

17

Each Patrol camps as a separate unit

Prefabricated Gadgets

These are all gadgets you can build before camp, possibly at your Patrol Meetings during winter.

This Patrol Box opens up to become a table and two benches.

900 mm

600 mm.

250mm

bolt

wing nut inside leg of stool

One bench is shown stored inside table.

Legs of one stool fit inside legs of other, and are bolted together through lower end of box.

The box closed.

The measurements are for guidance only, and you should vary them to suit your own needs.

The table in use.

Instant table top. Webbing may be tacked or stapled over and under alternately.

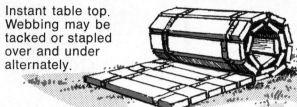

Shelf-box. Another way of utilising packing cases in camp.

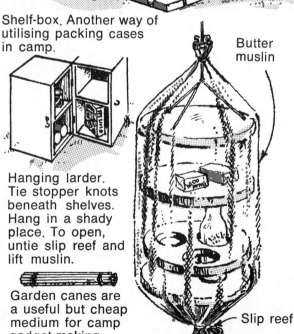

Butter muslin

Hanging larder. Tie stopper knots beneath shelves. Hang in a shady place. To open, untie slip reef and lift muslin.

Garden canes are a useful but cheap medium for camp gadget-making.

Slip reef

18

Hygiene

Emergency wash-bowl —plastic sheet over a ring of rocks.

Soaping or whitewashing the outside of billies before use on fire makes them easier to clean.

While you cook, have water boiling ready for washing up.

Camp Wash-Stand

Mirror →

Tins to hold toothbrushes

Plastic, or old groundsheet

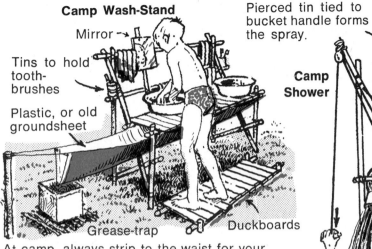

Pierced tin tied to bucket handle forms the spray.

Grease-trap

Duckboards

At camp, always strip to the waist for your morning wash.

Washing-up

Never leave all the washing-up until after the meal, or try to clean plates in lukewarm water.

When you serve a meal, wash the cooking pots before the grease goes hard.

Camp Shower

String around base leads up to pulley.

Line from holdfast allows shower to be lowered for filling.

Duckboards

This isn't a nudist camp, so hide your shower among bushes, or put up screens.

Waste Disposal

Ask landowner when you arrive what he will want done with rubbish.

Incinerator—a can with holes in, over fire. To punch holes, fill can with earth, use six inch nail or marline spike.

Traditional wet and dry pits

Grease-trap—strong cover of interlaced sticks and filter of grass, renewed daily.

Only thoroughly washed or burnt material in here. Never glass.

With the increasing demand on camp sites, the traditional dry pit is giving way to sacks or plastic bags in which washed or flattened tins may be stored until they can be taken home or to a convenient refuse dump.

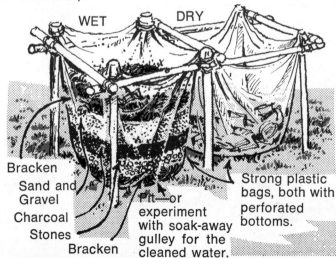

WET   DRY

Bracken
Sand and Gravel
Charcoal
Stones
Bracken

Pit—or experiment with soak-away gulley for the cleaned water.

Strong plastic bags, both with perforated bottoms.

Oil can, stuffed with grass, burnt daily.

Grid over soak-away pit.

Oil-can filter is easy to make and to maintain.

Empty Tin Cans

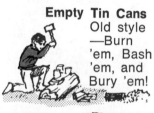

Old style —Burn 'em, Bash 'em, and Bury 'em!

New Style— CLEAN 'EM

CRUSH 'EM

AND CARRY 'EM HOME!

Camp Latrines

Toilet tent

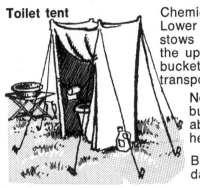

Chemical toilet. Lower bucket stows inside the upper bucket for transport.

Never let bucket fill above here.

Bucket is emptied daily into a pit.

Top view of layout for two-seater from one length of hessian.

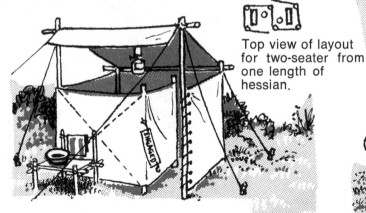

PATROL 'SUPER-LOO'. Anything which makes the camp latrine more convenient to use, contributes to the good health of all in camp.

Always wash hands after visiting the latrine, and AGAIN before handling food.

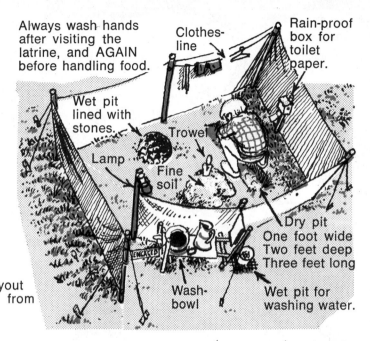

Clothes-line

Rain-proof box for toilet paper.

Wet pit lined with stones.

Trowel

Lamp

Fine soil

Dry pit
One foot wide
Two feet deep
Three feet long

Wash-bowl

Wet pit for washing water.

Some people prefer a free-standing seat over the pit.

All excrement must be covered completely with soil.

Toilet paper protected in plastic bag.

Pony Trekking

Pioneering

Swimming

Filming

Sailing

Gliding

Monkey Bridge

Scouter's Kitchen

Store

Beaver Patrol

Wind Direction

Seal Patrol

Life Saving Picket

22   Troop Camp is the base

Hiking

Magazine

Kingfisher Patrol

Scouters' Tent

First Aid Tent

Scout Vehicle Park

Main Latrine

Sightseeing

Camp Sports

Rafting

mit of safe wimming area

Botany

de range of activities

23

Flag Poles

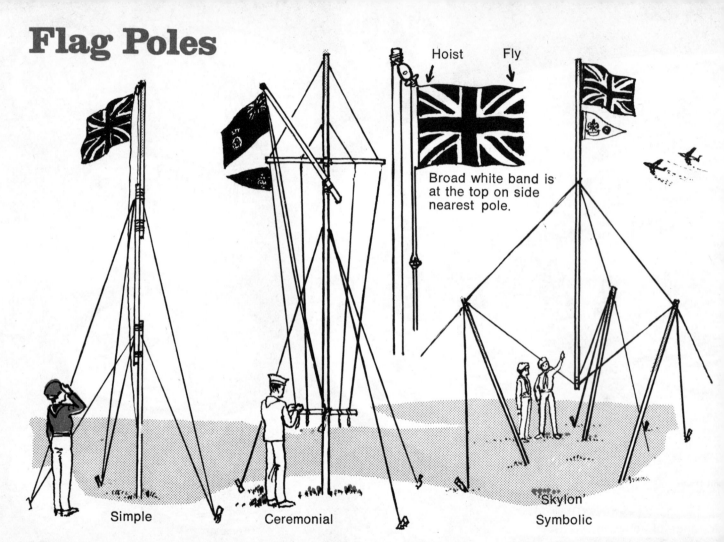

Hoist   Fly

Broad white band is at the top on side nearest pole.

Simple

Ceremonial

'Skylon' Symbolic

INSPECTION

Air your gear as soon as you get up. It should be well-aired and stowed away again by ten o'clock.

Patrol Leader checks: tent is properly pitched; any damp gear airing; clean kit packed in kit bags; bedding on line; food, plates, cooking gear clean and tidy; dress suitable for the day's activity.

Normal

Wet Day

Slacken guy-lines, store personal kit in bags, turn back groundsheet. Cover woodpile. Make sure no water can enter tent. Don't touch sides of tent. Get a good fire going. Wear bathing shorts or waterproofs.

Formal

Full uniform. All kit laid out, tent brailed, etc. Applies only on special occasions.

Patrol Leader checks that no gear has been left outside—nothing on the airing line. Slacken guys, cover woodpile, rake ash over embers of fire. No paraffin or gas lamps inside tent—only battery lamps. No day-time clothes worn in bed. All quiet at agreed time for 'lights out'.

Evening

Backwoods Camping & Cooking

Frame work for a natural shelter

thatched with reeds or long grass.

Two ways of making a shelter from a square of canvas.

Prepare a green stick to make a broiler, toasting-fork or skewer. Do NOT use laurel or yew.

Broiler.

Self-Raising flour and water will make a dough which may be toasted on a green stick.

A 'Kebab'— meat and vegetables on a skewer.

Eggs roasting in orange peel.

Apples on greenstick skewers.

'Fiji Oven'—Build a fire in a hole in the ground. Rake out the fire and stack as shown for six hours.

— Earth
— Cabbage leaves
— FOOD
— More leaves
— Hot stones
— Hot embers

Spud Egg
Large potato hollowed out and egg broken into it. Skewer back the top and roast in embers.

If you're careful you can even skewer an egg!

Plastic & Foil in Camp

1. Use foil to make a double-thickness envelope for food.

Improvise a tent from heavy-gauge polythene sheet and string.

Spread polythene cloth as tablecloth before you lay out food.

A frying pan made from a green forked stick and some foil.

Black polythene lining a hole in the ground gives both a wash basin and a mirror.

2. Seal edges tightly but leave room for air to expand.

3. Bury in hot embers —never in flaming fire.

Try folding foil to make— a container for boiling eggs.

1

2

3

No water-carrier? Put a large plastic bag in your rucsac, tying the top to stop water from slopping over.

At the end of Camp

1. Pay all camp bills by your last full day.

2. Take down all inessential gadgets.

3. Last morning: on getting up, pack all personal kit except uniform and what you have on.

4. Fold tents and bundle the poles securely together.

5. Clear field of all gear. Stack it as close as you can to the pick-up place.

6. Re-check activity areas and bushes around site for equipment or litter.

7. Form a line-up of whole Patrol walking slowly across camp site picking up tiny bits of litter, toffee papers.

8. Fill and re-turf all pits, leaving 'foul ground' signs where required.

9. Final wash; pack last of camp clothes; get changed into uniform.

10. Thank the landowner. Invite him to inspect the site before you leave.

11. When you get home, remember to thank the driver, your Scout Leader, your Patrol Leader, and your parents for letting you go.

12. Next day write to thank traders and friends you made at camp and tell them you reached home safely.

Hike Camping

When you have learnt to manage on a minimum of equipment, you may progress towards hike camps and expeditions.

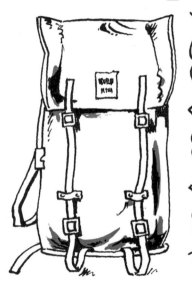

Waterproof
Hike tent
Stove

Food
Cutlery
Canteen

Clothes,
Sleeping-
bag

Anorak

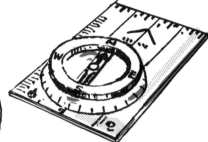

Skill in the use of map and compass is essential.

Wool, flannel, or canvas trousers.

Two pairs of thick wool socks.

Stout shoes or boots.

A large heavy-duty plastic bag with a hole cut for your face.

When packing a rucsac, always remember 'Last in—First out'.

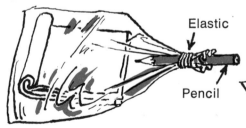

Elastic

Pencil

Wear woollen jersey and cap, cellular underwear and flannel shirt.

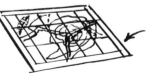

O.S. Map in plastic envelope, the edges bound with adhesive tape.

Cycle Camping

Finding the Easiest Route

Mark along the edge of a strip of paper the points where contour lines cross your route. Then draw a graph to show the relative steepness of gradients.

Before any expedition, check that your cycle is roadworthy and working efficiently.

Stow all your gear in balanced panniers, NOT on your back.

Never cycle more than two abreast. Drop to single file whenever cars are overtaking or the road narrows or bends sharply.

Collapsible water-carrier.

Groundsheet.

Stove, tent, pegs.

Spare clothes, sleeping bag, pyjamas.

Tool kit, torch, washing kit.

First Aid kit. Towel.

Food, canteen.

Poles lashed to back stays.

You can cover far more ground on wheels than on foot, but when you intend to set up camp each night fourteen miles per day is plenty.

Canoe Camping

TRAIN FOR A CANOE CHARGE CERTIFICATE BEFORE GOING ON A CRUISE.

All canoes must stay together.

Drip rings

Spray cover

Food and maps for the day's journey. Washing kit.

Tent

Sleeping bag

Spare clothes and pyjamas

Buoyancy

Life-jacket

Buoyancy

Fuel Stove Water

Repair and First Aid Kit

When you plan your route make sure that canoes are allowed on the river.

All your canoes must have an up-to-date Boat Certificate.

All the Scouts must have swum at least 50 metres in clothes.

Life Jackets must be worn. Always travel in groups of 3 or more.

Fold, tie and fold again . . .

or make a clamp from two wing-nuts.

Store all food, clothes and equipment in waterproof bags. Fold the opening down, and tie or clamp.

When packing your canoe, balance the weight. Secure all bags, especially those near the cockpit. Keep your legs and the cockpit opening clear of obstructions. Attach string to furthest bundles to help you to pull them out.

Camping Variations

Possible variations on the camping theme increase as you become more experienced.

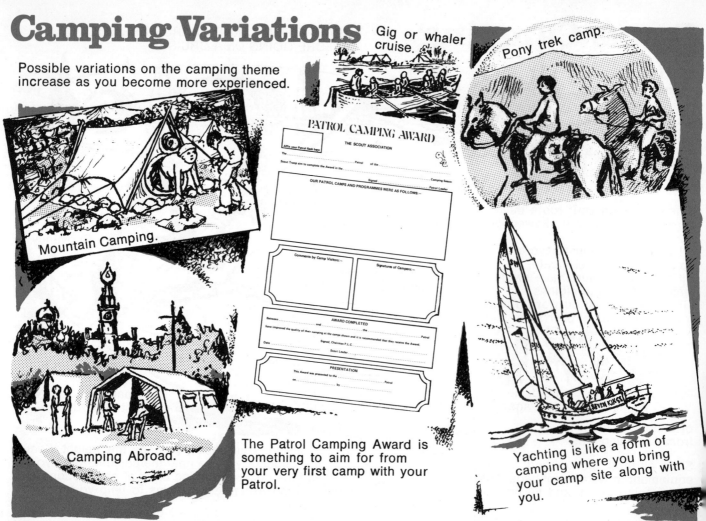

Gig or whaler cruise.

Pony trek camp.

Mountain Camping.

Camping Abroad.

The Patrol Camping Award is something to aim for from your very first camp with your Patrol.

Yachting is like a form of camping where you bring your camp site along with you.

PATROL CAMPING AWARD

THE SCOUT ASSOCIATION

OUR PATROL CAMPS AND PROGRAMMES WERE AS FOLLOWS:—

Comments by Camp Visitors:—

Signatures of Campers:—

AWARD COMPLETED

PRESENTATION